The Little Book of
SHELLS

**BUSHEL
& PECK
BOOKS**

Bushel & Peck Books is dedicated to fighting illiteracy all over the world.
For every book we sell, we donate one to a child in need—book for book.
To nominate a school or organization to receive free books,
please visit www.bushelandpeckbooks.com.

Type set in Temeraire, Avenir Next, and Bebas.

Illustrations sourced from the Biodiversity Heritage Library and Graphics Fairy. Other
image credits as follows: shell pattern: Daniela Iga/Shutterstock.com; shell icon: Original
Logo/Shutterstock.com; graph paper background: Vector Image Plus/Shutterstock.com.
Animal taxonomy sourced from Wikipedia.

LCCN: 2022934187
ISBN: 9781638190073

First Edition

Printed in the United States

10 9 8 7 6 5 4 3 2 1

The Little Book of
SHELLS

CHRISTIN FARLEY

CONTENTS

1. LIMPET

Limpets are a type of sea snail belonging to the *Patellidae* family. They are usually less than three inches long and have cone-shaped shells with ridges that reach to the apex. They usually attach themselves to rocks, where they use their radula to scrape algae from the rock's surface. The radula is a tiny, ribbon-shaped tongue with minute teeth. While limpets like to snack on algae, *they're* snacks for other predators, including starfish, seals, and even humans. Limpets spawn once a year when the waters are rough, usually in winter, and their eggs and sperm are dispersed by the water. Amazingly, limpets on bare rocks can live up to sixteen years!

CLASSIFICATION

KINGDOM: *Animalia*

PHYLUM: *Mollusca*

CLASS: *Gastropoda*

SUBCLASS: *Patellogastropoda*

WHERE TO FIND THEM
Limpets are found along rocky shorelines where the tide comes in and out. These places are called intertidal zones. They can be found in most waters worldwide, except for the arctic seas. While they live alone, they do tend to be near other limpets.

STAY ON THE TRAIL

Limpets are on the move when the tide is in, shuffling around the rocks in a localized area. However, when the tide goes out, they return to their favorite spot following a mucus trail they've left behind. Coming back to the same spot over and over causes a "home scar," or a trail-like indentation, on the rock.

GOOD GRIP

If you ever find a limpet at a tide pool, you'll notice it is there to stay! The limpet's grip on the rock is so strong that a naval mine was named after it and called a "Limpet mine." These mines stick to targets like magnets. Trying to remove a limpet from its rock will likely damage its muscles, so it's best to leave it be.

2. CERITH

The cerith is an abundant, small marine snail that grows to be only an inch in length. Sometimes referred to as a "horned shell," a cerith's shell is spiraled and narrow with a pointy tip. This marine gastropod is part of the *Cerithiidae* family and has more than 300 known species. A cerith's main food source is algae and marine waste. Its radula (tongue) has seven teeth in each row that allow it to scrape up food, like algae, off of rocks. Some ceriths are nocturnal and bury themselves in the sand during the day. This behavior also happens when there are rough water conditions.

CLASSIFICATION

KINGDOM: *Animalia*

PHYLUM: *Mollusca*

CLASS: *Gastropoda*

SUBCLASS: *Caenogastropoda*

SUPERFAMILY: *Cerithioidea*

FAMILY: *Cerithiidae*

WHERE TO FIND THEM

Ceriths are found in shallow waters worldwide, though they are more prevalent in the tropics. You can find them on coral reef rocks, sandy bottoms, and reef flats. The Baja Peninsula alone is home to forty-two of the cerith species.

AQUARIUM ALL-STARS

Ceriths are peaceful, hardworking snails and a favorite among aquarium hobbyists. They are a popular choice because of their ability to scavenge and keep tanks clean. They will eat unwanted algae and fish feces, all while keeping the peace with other tank residents.

CLEAN-UP CREW

How many ceriths are needed to keep a tank clean? The usual rule of thumb is to have one cerith for every five or ten gallons of water. If too many are added, the ceriths might die of starvation—there's only so much algae to go around!

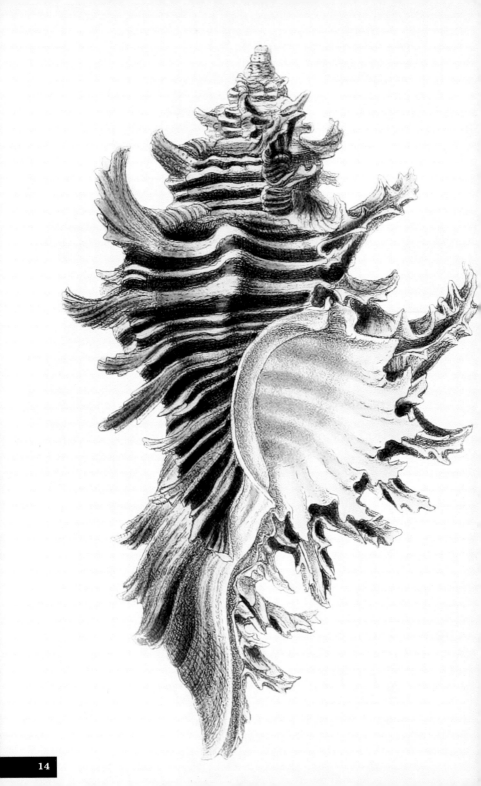

3. MUREX

A murex is a large, predatory, tropical sea snail. It is commonly called a "rock snail" and is part of the *Muricidae* family. This gastropod mollusk is easily identified by its spiky, irregular exterior. Murex shells are known for being ornate on the outside and brightly colored on the inside. While they have beautiful shells, their method of hunting might seem barbaric in comparison! A murex drills a hole through the shell of another shelled animal (like clams or oysters), sticks in its proboscis (its nose), and ingests the soft insides of its prey.

CLASSIFICATION

KINGDOM: *Animalia*

PHYLUM: *Mollusca*

CLASS: *Gastropoda*

SUBCLASS: *Caenogastropoda*

ORDER: *Neogastropoda*

FAMILY: *Muricidae*

SUBFAMILY: *Muricinae*

GENUS: *Murex*

WHERE TO FIND THEM

Murexes can be found in tropical regions on rocky or sandy bottoms, near intertidal zones and coral, or along the water's shore.

15

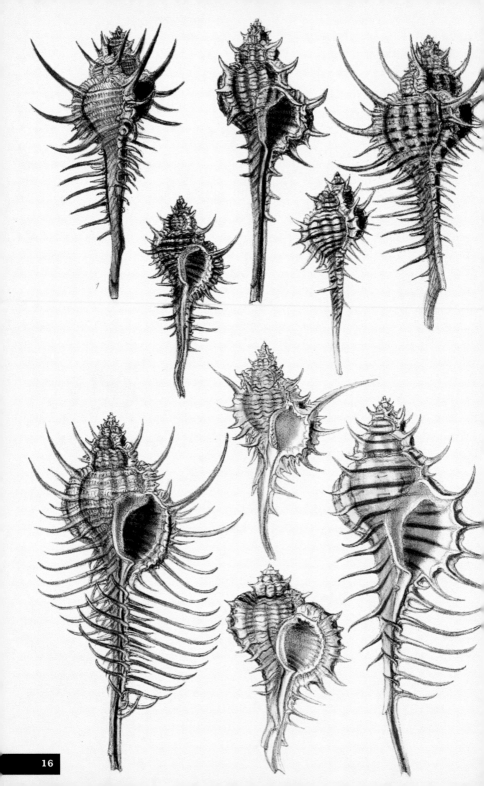

ANCIENT ANCESTRY

There are about 1,600 living species in the Muricidae *family worldwide. According to fossil records, these snail varieties have existed for more than 3.6 million years.*

MONEY-MAKING MUCUS

In the ancient world, some murex species were used to create a rare, expensive purple dye from the murex's mucus. Called "Tyrian purple," this luxurious color was used mainly for royalty.

4. OLIVE SHELL

O live shells have a glossy, smooth feel and a bullet-shaped design. They are long and narrow with a spiral just on the tip. Inside is a carnivorous sea snail that is part of the *Olividae* family. They are normally small but can grow to just over two inches in length. Relying on their sense of smell, buried olive shells will reach from under the sand with their large fleshy foot, drag their prey under the sand, and then smother it with mucus. Victims usually include small crustaceans, other snails, and decaying fish. What a way to hunt!

CLASSIFICATION

KINGDOM: *Animalia*

PHYLUM: *Mollusca*

CLASS: *Gastropoda*

SUBCLASS: *Caenogastropoda*

ORDER: *Neogastropoda*

SUPERFAMILY: *Olivoidea*

FAMILY: *Olividae*

WHERE TO FIND THEM

Olive shells are found worldwide but more commonly in tropical and subtropical oceans. Look for them during low tide and at night, as they prefer to burrow in the sand during the day.

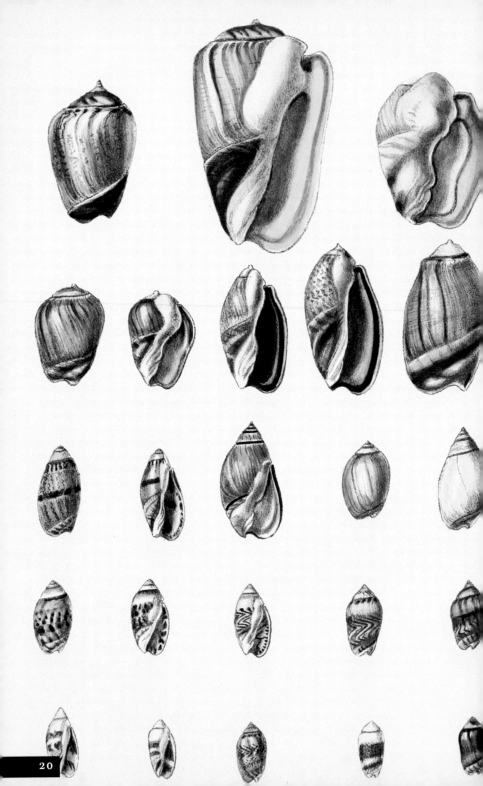

TINY HOMES

Once a host snail has died, its seashell often makes a great home for a hermit crab. The olive shell is one of the exceptions; its shape leaves simply not enough room for a hermit crab to live comfortably!

TRAILBLAZERS

If you are wondering where an olive shell disappears to after it burrows under the sand, just look at the surface. Olive shells leave a trail of raised sand in whatever direction they choose to go.

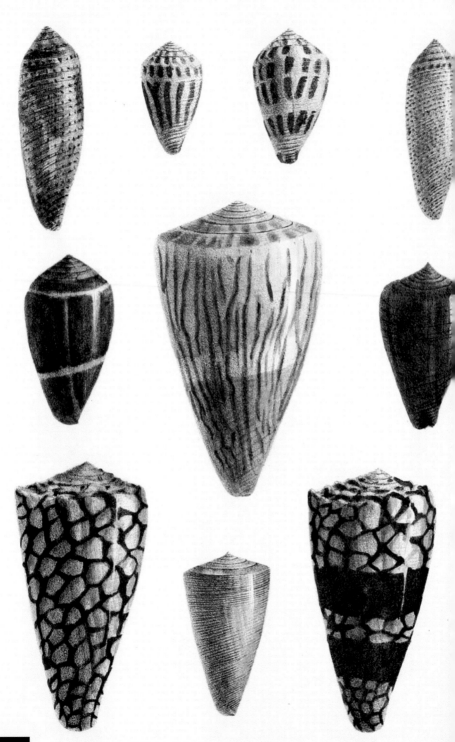

5. CONE SHELL

Cone shells are predatory creatures with strikingly beautiful shells designed with a brown and white net pattern. The largest of the cone shells can grow up to nine inches in length! They belong to the family *Conidae* and make up over 500 species. When hunting for food, they are known to sting with a harpoon-like tooth, which paralyzes their prey. The cone then reels the prey back in with its proboscis, eating it whole. Cone shells are, in fact, one of the most venomous creatures in the world, and the stings of the larger species can even go through a glove or a wetsuit. Stings from a smaller cone are comparable to a bee sting, but a larger cone's sting can be lethal. Not looking for human conflict, cones typically only sting when handled by deep reef divers. But if you see a living cone shell, it's best to leave it be!

CLASSIFICATION

KINGDOM: *Animalia*

PHYLUM: *Mollusca*

CLASS: *Gastropoda*

SUBCLASS: *Caenogastropoda*

ORDER: *Neogastropoda*

SUPERFAMILY: *Conoidea*

FAMILY: *Conidae*

GENUS: *Conus*

WHERE TO FIND THEM

Cone shells can be found off the coast of Florida, the Indian and Pacific oceans, and the Caribbean and Red seas. They are most commonly found in shallow waters near coral reefs.

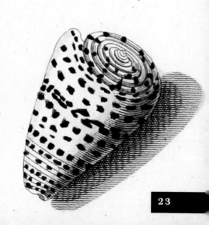

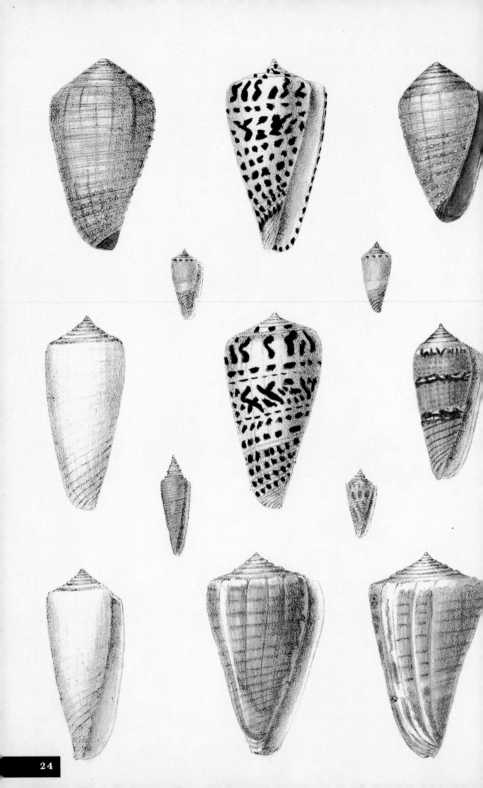

FAST AND FURIOUS

The strike of a cone shell is one of the fastest in the animal kingdom. Its attack on its prey takes only milliseconds, leaving no chance for the sea worm or small fish to escape.

NOT ALL BAD

Though cone shells are venemous predators, scientists have found a promising protein in their venom compounds that could be used as an effective pain killer. It might even help prevent epileptic seizures.

6. MOON SNAIL

CLASSIFICATION

KINGDOM: *Animalia*

PHYLUM: *Mollusca*

CLASS: *Gastropoda*

SUBCLASS: *Caenogastropoda*

ORDER: *Littorinimorpha*

FAMILY: *Naticidae*

Also called "necklace shells," moon snails are part of the *Naticidae* family. Their shells have a globular shape and get their name from the half-moon shaped openings on one side. Like many ocean snails, the moon snail burrows into the sand, where it spends most of its time hiding from predators. At night, it comes out to hunt for other snails and mollusks. It uses its foot to move along the sand and later to suffocate its prey (it's a tough world down there!). While an efficient predator itself, a moon shell can also make a good meal for hunting gulls and humans alike.

WHERE TO FIND THEM

Moon snails are found worldwide in sandy intertidal areas from the tropics to the arctic regions. The largest moon snail, called the Lewis' moon snail, can be found on the North American coast from Alaska to southern California. They can also be found off the coast of Japan.

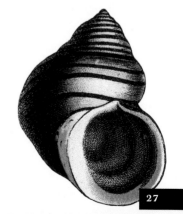

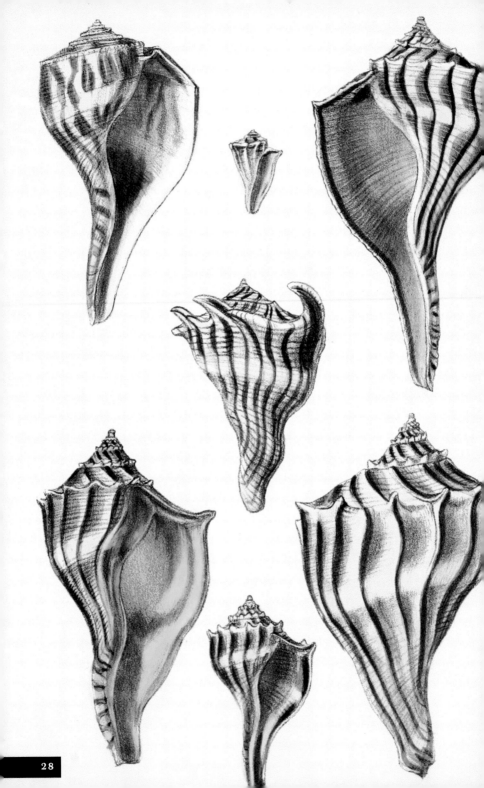

7. WHELK

There are over fifty species of whelk in the *Buccinidae* family. The most popular include the knobbed, channeled, rapa, and lightning whelks. Whelks are some of the largest snails in the sea and can range from one inch in length to over two feet! They are sometimes mistakenly called conches. You can identify a whelk shell by its spiral and textured knobs. Tropical species tend to be smaller and more colorful than their cold-water counterparts. Like other marine snails, whelks use their muscular foot to move and to hold their prey when hunting for clams, mussels, and oysters.

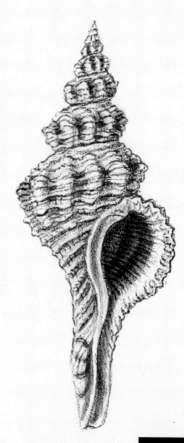

WHERE TO FIND THEM

Whelks can be found in most areas of the world in either tropical or cold-water seas. Most commonly, they are found in the North Atlantic and along the coastlines of Europe and North America in sandy bottoms at ocean depths of up to 650 feet.

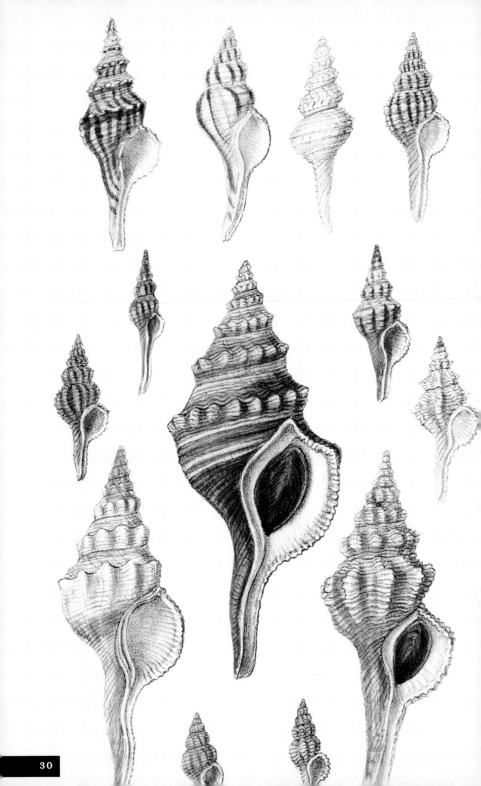

SANDY SURPRISE

Have you ever found what you thought was a snakeskin on the beach? Chances are, it was an empty whelk egg casing. The spiral-shaped casings can reach thirty-three inches in length. When in use, a female whelk fills them with around 200 small pouches, each with up to ninety-nine eggs inside!

STRONG SNIFFER

Common whelks locate their food with something called a siphon. This tube-like structure has chemoreceptors that allow whelks to "smell" the water. With a sweep of the siphon, the whelk can detect nearby food and even distinguish the smell of predators. When the whelk picks up the scent of prey, it can move up to five inches per minute to close in on its meal. Not lightning, but fast enough!

8. TURBAN

Turbans are marine snails that belong to the *Turbinidae* family. A turban is characterized by its conical shape and large aperture (opening) in the first whorl. The largest species is the green turban, which can reach up to eight inches in length. More common, however, are the brown and black turban shells, which are closer to one inch. Predators include other snails, octopuses, and rock crabs. When fleeing from a predator—and if they're lucky enough to be on a sloping surface—black turbans are quick thinkers. They climb on the opposing snail's shell or, most fun of all, detach themselves and roll down the rocky intertidal slope! When turbans' long lives of five to eight years end, hermit crabs are happy to inhabit their vacant shells.

CLASSIFICATION

KINGDOM: *Animalia*

PHYLUM: *Mollusca*

CLASS: *Gastropoda*

SUBCLASS: *Vetigastropoda*

ORDER: *Trochida*

SUPERFAMILY: *Trochoidea*

FAMILY: *Turbinidae*

WHERE TO FIND THEM

Green turbans are native to Australia and the East Indies, while brown and black turbans inhabit North American shorelines, from British Columbia to Mexico. Turbans make their homes in rocky intertidal zones, where they can congregate on boulders and in crevices.

9. TOP SHELL

Like its name implies, a top is a marine snail that can resemble the spinning toy. The conical shell is known for its rhombic opening and flat base. Members of the *Trochidae* family, top shells are related to kelp shells and periwinkles and include hundreds of species. Some common species are the zebra, ribbed, and wavy top shells. These social snails prefer to live gregariously (in groups) near food sources. Tops are herbivores and can be found in shallow water on rocks covered with delicious algae, which they scrape off with their radula.

CLASSIFICATION

KINGDOM: *Animalia*

PHYLUM: *Mollusca*

CLASS: *Gastropoda*

SUBCLASS: *Vetigastropoda*

ORDER: *Trochida*

SUPERFAMILY: *Trochoidea*

FAMILY: *Calliostomatidae*

SUBFAMILY: *Calliostomatinae*

GENUS: *Calliostoma*

WHERE TO FIND THEM

Top shells can be found throughout the ocean, from the deep open seas to intertidal zones. They're most diverse in rocky shores and shallow waters and can be found near the equator all the way to high latitudes with colder water.

INNER GLITZ

All top shells have beautiful, nacreous (iridescent) interiors. The largest species of top shell, the Trochus niloticus, *was once extensively fished for its lustrous pearl-like coating in the Indo-Pacific region. Its interior was later used to manufacture pearl buttons. They are still harvested and sold today for crafts and nautical home decor.*

LOOK-ALIKES

Top shells can be easily confused with turban shells. There are a couple ways to tell them apart. The operculum (or trap door) is thin on a top shell and is made of a horn-like material; if you turn a turban upside down, you'll see that its operculum is thick and rounded. The other difference is in the muscular foot: only the top shell has tentacles on its foot.

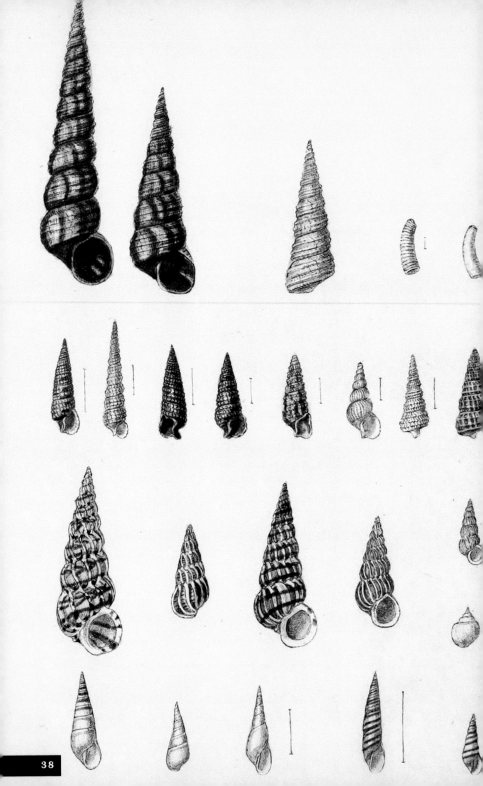

10. TURRET

CLASSIFICATION

KINGDOM: *Animalia*

PHYLUM: *Mollusca*

CLASS: *Gastropoda*

SUBCLASS: *Caenogastropoda*

SUPERFAMILY: *Cerithioidea*

FAMILY: *Turritellidae*

GENUS: *Turritella*

You might know them as "tower shells" or "screw shells," which makes sense because turret shells have many whorls and a narrow, elongated shape. Part of the *Turritellidae* family, turret shells are an exciting find along your walk on the shore! The inner marine snail is a suspension feeder. This means that it uses its ciliated gill filaments to filter particles of ocean waste and debris out of the water. These nocturnal snails are generally about one to five inches in length and burrow into the sand for protection. Turrets are a favorite snack among other animals, like fish, crabs, birds, and other predatory snails.

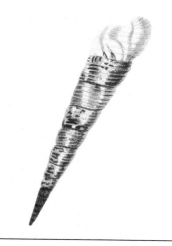

WHERE TO FIND THEM

Turrets are found worldwide in all temperate waters and tropical seas. Of their nearly 200 species, seventeen types of turrents are found in the waters of North America. Turrets are known to live in large colonies in intertidal zones and shallow water, though these are sometimes as deep down as 4,900 feet.

CLOSE-UP CONSIDERATIONS

How can you tell the difference between a turret and other long shells, like the auger and miter? With a careful eye, you can distinguish the turret by the following traits: 1) a non-lustrous and rough exterior, 2) no siphonal canal, and 3) whorls in a convex shape.

IN-HOUSE HELPERS

Like other marine snails, the turret is an important and necessary addition to a clean home aquarium. Turret snails do an outstanding job of consuming organic, decaying material and help keep water healthy for all inhabitants. They also add character and beauty to a tank with their spiraling shell designs!

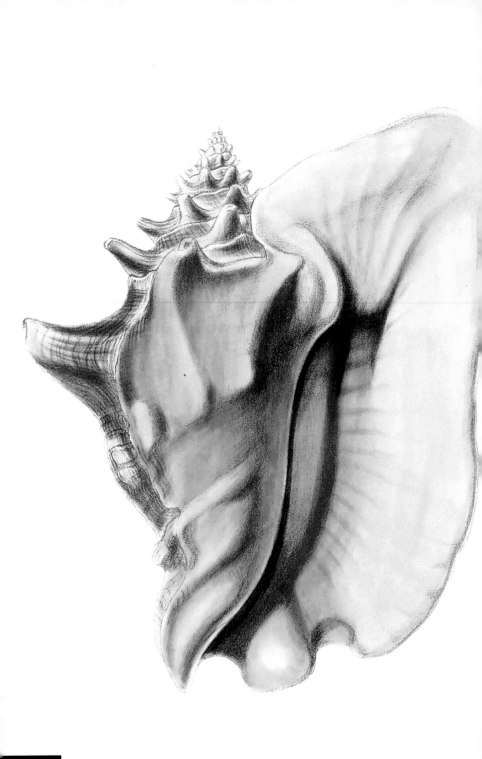

11. CONCH

There are certain seashells that are simply iconic, and the shell of the conch snail is just that! This predatory marine gastropod has a medium to large colorful, ornate shell and a high, curled spire. Some varieties also have knobbed spines on top and a flared and thick outer lip. Though rare, a conch can sometimes even produce pearls inside its shell. Depending on the environment, the pearls might be pink, white, brown, or even orange. These amazing creatures can live around thirty years and can be both herbivorous and carnivorous, depending on the type. Even with their strong, thick shells, the conch can still fall prey to other snails, who bore a hole through the shell, and to various species of octopus.

CLASSIFICATION

KINGDOM: *Animalia*

PHYLUM: *Mollusca*

CLASS: *Gastropoda*

SUBCLASS: *Caenogastropoda*

ORDER: *Littorinimorpha*

SUPERFAMILY: *Stromboidea*

FAMILY: *Strombidae*

WHERE TO FIND THEM

Native to Bermuda, the Bahamas, the Florida Keys, and the Caribbean, conch shells live throughout the world in tropical waters. They're often found among reefs, seagrass beds, and shallow reefs.

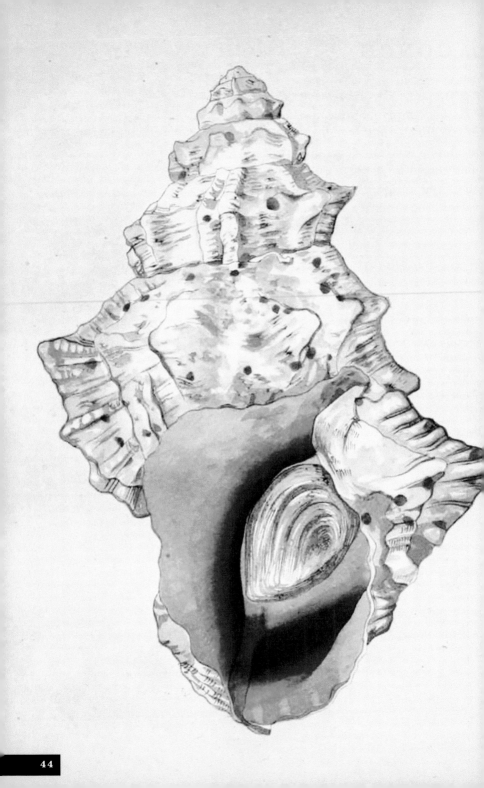

INTRIGUING INSTRUMENT

For centuries, the conch shell has been used as an instrument in Japan, Korea, Malta, and the Caribbean. In the music world, it is part of the wind family. To turn the shell into an instrument, a hole is drilled in the shell's spire close to the apex, which is the oldest part of the shell. To produce sound, a person blows through the hole. Not surprisingly, another name for the conch is the "shell trumpet."

A MUST-TRY MEAL

If you take a trip to the Bahamas, make sure to try one of their most popular dishes: conch! It can be found in almost any restaurant and is similar to calamari (squid). Try conch steamed, deep-fried, or as a part of another dish or soup. With a firm and somewhat chewy texture, you can discover what the locals are raving about!

FAST FILTERING

Oysters are incredibly efficient by cleaning the water around them while they eat.
As oysters draw in water over their gills, their tiny hairs trap plankton and other particles, drawing it to its mouth. Through this process, they remove excess algae and sediments from the water. In fact, one oyster can filter fifty gallons of water a day! They are key to a healthy marine ecosystem.

12. OYSTER

Oysters are mollusks that are both plump and rich in nutrients. They belong to the *Ostreidae* family and are characterized by their rough, irregular, oval shells. While all oysters can produce pearls, they are not usually the pretty, perfectly round pearls you might think of. Oysters have been around for millions of years and have played an important role in many cultures. Curiously, oysters can change their gender throughout their lives. They usually begin as males and often change to females the next season. Sadly, of all marine habitats on earth, oyster reefs are among the most threatened; already, 85-90% of oyster reefs have been lost in the wild. Thanks to restoration projects, efforts are being made to reverse this problem.

CLASSIFICATION

KINGDOM: *Animalia*

PHYLUM: *Mollusca*

CLASS: *Bivalvia*

SUBCLASS: *Pteriomorphia*

WHERE TO FIND THEM

Oysters are found in waters worldwide, except for Antarctica. Brackish water (a mix of fresh and salty water) from estuaries makes a thriving habitat where oysters can be partially protected by land. Here, they adhere to rocks and other oysters in water depths between two and twenty-six feet.

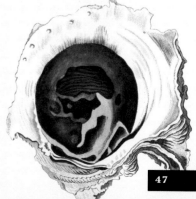

13. MUSSEL

When it comes to mussels, there is a lot of variety! While they generally have a blue-black colored shell and a length of about two to three inches, mussels come in many more shapes and sizes. Mussels are divided into two groups: marine mussels, which belong to the *Mytilidae* family, and freshwater mussels, which belong to the *Unionidae* family. For more than 20,000 years, mussels have been a food source for humans. The size of the mussel depends on the season. They are smallest in March; in October, they reach their prime. Unlike other marine mollusks, you can tell the difference between male and female mussels just by looking at their mantle colors. Females have orange mantles, while males have white.

WHERE TO FIND THEM

Almost any body of water can contain mussels, from streams and creeks to estuaries and along the coastline. Mussels can even be found in Antarctica!

49

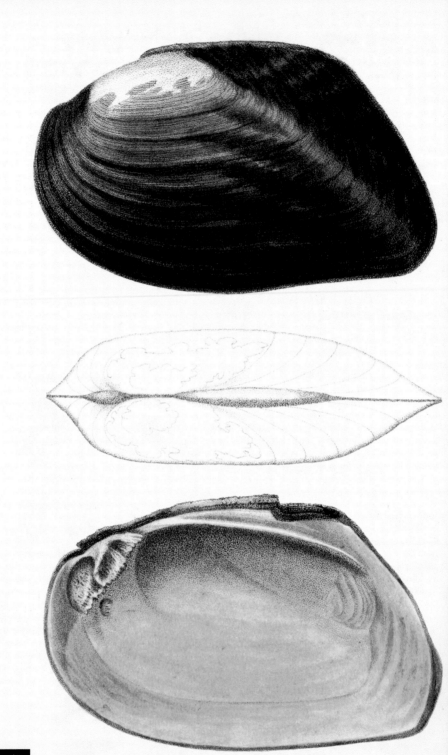

MIGHTY MUSSELS

If mussels had a superpower, it would be their byssus thread—a fine, silky thread that allows them to adhere to rocks and other surfaces. Their "superglue" even sticks to Teflon! (That's the non-stick coating on many pans and skillets.) Scientists are exploring how to use this as a way to close surgical wounds and speed healing.

HEALTHY ALTERNATIVE

Mussels are jam-packed with nutrition. As a beef alternative, mussels are rich in protein, have far less fat, have more mineral nutrients, and have only a quarter of the calories. Like beef, they have to be cooked, but they can be steamed or pan fried to create a variety of amazing recipes!

14. CLAM

Clams are a species of bivalve mollusks. All bivalves, like clams, oysters, mussels, and scallops, have two hinged shells. The intersting thing about clams, though, is that these small, edible creatures have a heart, mouth, kidneys, stomach, and even a simple nervous system. Clams are oval in shape. Their hinge is made from strong adductor muscles that connect their two equal halves of shell. A clam's powerful foot allows it to burrow under the sand or mud. To eat, clams siphon water through their bodies and catch microscopic organisms in their gills. These filter feeders enjoy plankton and algae.

CLASSIFICATION

KINGDOM: *Animalia*

PHYLUM: *Mollusca*

CLASS: *Bivalvia*

INFRACLASS: *Heteroconchia*

SUBTERCLASS: *Euheterodonta*

SUPERORDER: *Imparidentia*

ORDER: *Venerida*

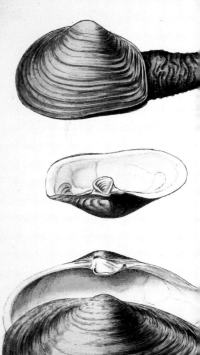

WHERE TO FIND THEM

Clams live in both marine and fresh water habitats all over the world. The greatest variety of saltwater clams can be found in North America. Clams often live in shallow water along river shores and seacoasts, but some species live freely on the seafloor or can even burrow down eleven inches into the sand!

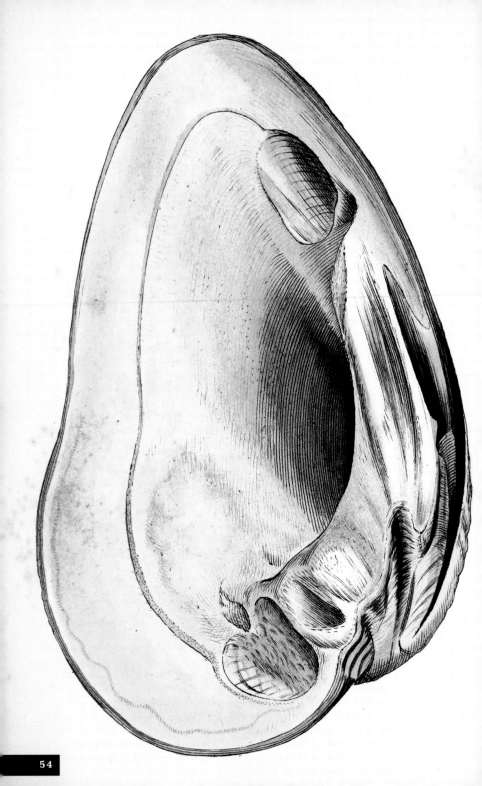

HEAVYWEIGHT CHAMPION

Of the 15,000 varieties of clam, the largest and most famous is the giant clam, or Tridacna gigas. *The giant clam can be found in the Indian Ocean and South Pacific waters. This behemoth can live for over 100 years and weigh more than 500 pounds. Now that's a real giant!*

HAPPY DIGGING

If clams burrow in wet sand, how do you know where to find them? One way is to look for little holes in the sand after the waves go out. If water is spurting out of the hole, then it's possible a clam is directly below. Some species only dig a half inch under the sand and can easily be unearthed.

15. SCALLOP

Scallops are a type of bivalve shellfish belonging to the *Pectinidae* family. There are more than 400 scallop species found worldwide with an estimated total scallop population of 40 billion! (Yep, that's with a "b.") Scallops can live as long as twenty years, and you can tell a scallop's age by counting the annuli (rings) on its shell—just like tree rings. Being filter feeders, scallops eat small organisms like plankton, and their diet determines the color of their shells; they can be a whole rainbow of colors! Scallops cannot burrow and dig like clams, but they can swim. They also use their shells as camouflage. Predators include lobster, crabs, and fish, but a scallop's chief enemy is the sea star.

CLASSIFICATION

KINGDOM: *Animalia*

PHYLUM: *Mollusca*

CLASS: *Bivalvia*

ORDER: *Pectinida*

SUPERFAMILY: *Pectinoidea*

FAMILY: *Pectinidae*

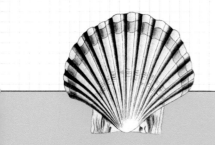

WHERE TO FIND THEM

Scallops can live in a wide variety of conditions but are most commonly found in shallow marine waters and seabeds. One species in particular, the Antarctic Scallop, is endemic to Antarctic waters, but like its other family members, it lives at depths above 300 feet. The largest number of scallop species live in the Indo-Pacific region.

EASY ON THE EYES

Scallops can have up to two hundred deep-blue eyes along the edge of their shells. Scientists are still learning about these eyes, which appear to function more like a telescope with mirrors (as opposed to human eyes, which focus light to the retina). But we do know that scallop eyes are proficient at detecting light and movement, which might help them evade predators.

SWIFT SWIMMERS

They might not make it to the Olympics, but scallops are athletic swimmers! They can cover a distance of five body lengths every second and are the only bivalve mollusk that is free swimming. To propel themselves forward (or away from predators), they quickly open and close their shells with their strong adductor muscles.

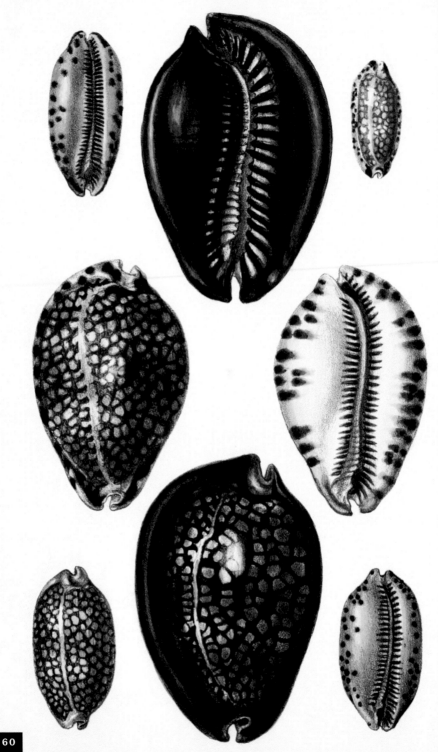

16. COWRY

Cowries are a group of sea snails known for their oblong egg shape and hard, smooth surface. Depending on which of the 200 species you find, they can range from the size of a thumbnail to the size of your palm. As a safety precaution, cowries hide in their shell by day and hunt for algae and detritus (waste) by night. Members of the *Cypraeidae* family, cowries are slippery and difficult for predators to reach because they have only a narrow-toothed slip in their shell. Slow moving, cowries don't cover much ground. They are one of few marine snails where the female will sit on her eggs. She covers them for several weeks with her muscular foot until they hatch.

CLASSIFICATION

KINGDOM: *Animalia*

PHYLUM: *Mollusca*

CLASS: *Gastropoda*

SUBCLASS: *Caenogastropoda*

ORDER: *Littorinimorpha*

SUPERFAMILY: *Cypraeoidea*

FAMILY: *Cypraeidae*

WHERE TO FIND THEM

Cowries are typically found in the tropical waters of the Indian and Pacific Oceans from Africa to Hawaii. They prefer hidden places, like under rocks in coral reefs. Warmer waters produce larger cowries. You can find some smaller varieties in the cooler waters of the British and European coasts.

ANCIENT ARTIFACTS

Cowries played an important role in ancient Fijian culture. Chieftains wore them on a necklace to show their rank and status.

FANCY FINISH

How do cowries keep their shells so polished and smooth while living in rough coral reefs? The answer is in their mantles. Cowries cover themselves up with fleshy members that extend from each side of the cowrie's slit and meet in the middle on the top of the shell. The mantles, often brightly colored, continue to lay down layers of protective enamel.

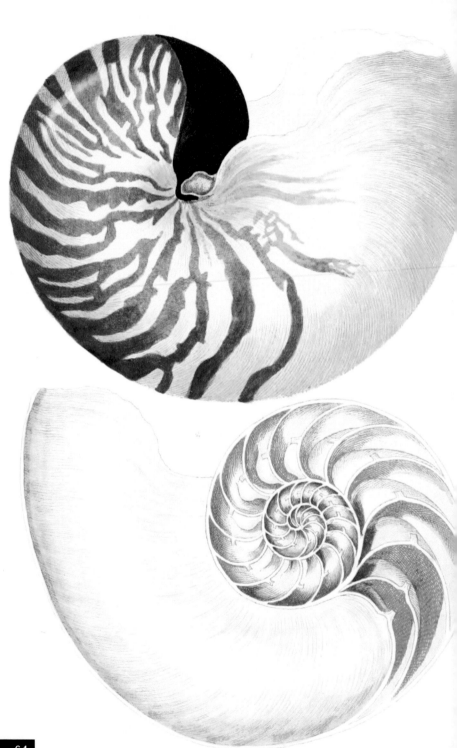

17. NAUTILUS

The nautilus is a predatory mollusk that resembles an octopus-like creature stuffed into a seashell. Although it is a cephalopod (like an octopus or squid), it is in a family all its own called *Nautilidae*. There were once believed to be thousands of species anciently, but only six are known to exist today. One of a nautilus's unique features is that its many inner chambers are filled with gas, which allows for buoyancy in the water to swim sideways, backwards, and forwards. These one-of-a-kind sea creatures may not have good eyesight, but their jet propulsion and sense of smell can help them catch crabs, shrimp, or carrion.

CLASSIFICATION

KINGDOM: *Animalia*

PHYLUM: *Mollusca*

CLASS: *Cephalopoda*

SUBCLASS: *Nautiloidea*

ORDER: *Nautilida*

SUPERFAMILY: *Nautilaceae*

FAMILY: *Nautilidae*

WHERE TO FIND THEM

All six species of nautilus reside in the Indo-Pacific region, though each species can vary slightly in distribution. (For instance, one species might only be found in New Guinea, while another only in the waters of Indonesia). Nautiluses like to inhabit coral reefs with deep slopes and drop offs. They are only found above 2,000 feet and in waters with temperatures below 75° Fahrenheit.

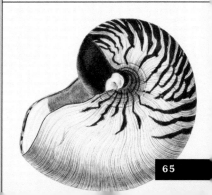

FAMILY RESEMBLANCE

While it's true that the nautilus has similarities to other cephalopods, there are a couple big differences (and it's not just the giant shell around its body!). A nautilus can have up to ninety tentacles, as opposed to the simple eight of their cephalopod cousins. And instead of suckers on its tentacles, a nautilus's tentacles are lined with ridges and grooves, allowing it to grip objects and pass them to its mouth.

LONG LIVE THE NAUTILUS!

Most cephalopods have a relatively short lifespan. The longest living octopus, for example, is the Pacific octopus, which can live up to five years (similar to most squid species). Incredibly, the nautilus can live to be a staggering twenty years old—or older!

Tusk Shell

18. TUSK

Tusk shells are marine mollusks with a shell that resembles an elephant tusk. However, unlike a true ivory tusk, this shell is open on both ends and buries itself in the sand. The wider end of the shell points downward, while the narrow end sticks above the sand to exchange water and expel waste. The scaphopod will attach inside its shell and reach its foot out the bottom. Tusks can move with surprising speed through loose sediment to escape predators, though the mature tusk will usually live its entire life buried in the substrate. A tusk's shell is on the small side with a typical length of one to two inches.

CLASSIFICATION

KINGDOM: *Animalia*

PHYLUM: *Mollusca*

SUBPHYLUM: *Conchifera*

CLASS: *Scaphopoda*

WHERE TO FIND THEM

Tusks are not fans of intertidal waters. While a few species can be found in shallow waters, the majority thrive in waters up to 5,000 feet deep. You can find them in muddy, soft ocean floors in warm and cool waters worldwide.

19. CHITON

Also known as "coat-of-mail shells" or "sea cradles," chitons are marine mollusks and make up around 1,000 known species. Unlike marine snails, chitons are protected with a series of eight overlapping shell plates (or valves) that look like armor. Around the entire shell is a leathery structure known as a girdle, which keeps the plates in place. On the underside of the chiton is the muscular foot, similar to other mollusks, which allows the chiton to move and grip surfaces. If, for some reason, the chiton becomes unattached, the flexible plates allow it to roll up in a ball for protection against sea stars, crabs, and gulls.

WHERE TO FIND THEM

Chitons chiefly reside in the intertidal zone, though a few species can live as deep as 20,000 feet. Found only in marine waters, chitons live throughout the world in warm, cold, and tropical seas. The giant chitons are found from southern California up to the western Alaskan coast in areas with abundant kelp.

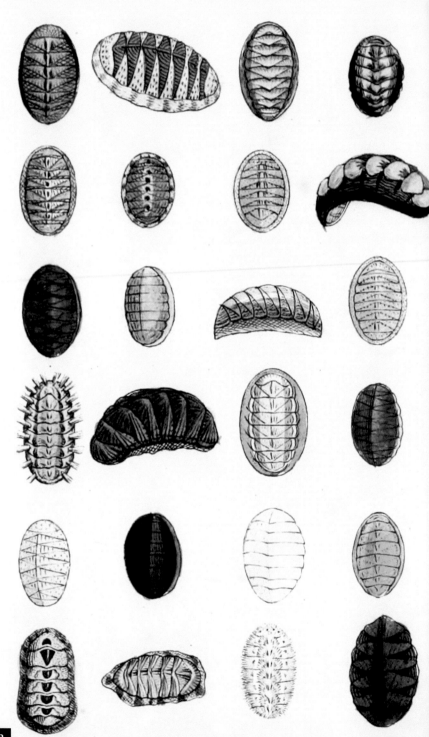

ALGAE SCRAPERS

Like many mollusks in this book, each chiton has a tongue-like structure called a radula. With rows and rows of teeth, the radula is used to scrape algae from rocks. Algae, of course, is one of a chiton's major food sources.

JUMBO GUMBO

The gumboot chiton is the largest species of chiton in the world. While the average chiton grows to be about two inches in length, the gumboot can reach up to thirteen inches! Not only that, but these chitons also have a longer lifespan of around twenty to twenty-five years. They have a reddish-brown color and only move about sixty-five feet every year.

20. ABALONE

One of the most prized finds in the ocean is the abalone. It is not only desired for its thick, iridescent shell, but also for its gourmet culinary uses. Abalone belong to the *Haliotidae* family and are sometimes called "sea ears" because of their flattened shells. Like other marine snails, abalone have a muscular foot that allows them to move about and cling tenaciously to rough surfaces. Algae and kelp are an abalone's main food sources. On the flipside, abalone are one of the first things sea otters look for in a new habitat—they aren't just tasty to humans! Due to natural predation and overharvesting, abalone have become rare and expensive. Some countries are attempting to farm them to create a sustainable seafood option.

CLASSIFICATION

KINGDOM: *Animalia*

PHYLUM: *Mollusca*

CLASS: *Gastropoda*

SUBCLASS: *Vetigastropoda*

ORDER: *Lepetellida*

FAMILY: *Haliotidae*

GENUS: *Haliotis*

WHERE TO FIND THEM
The majority of the world's abalone are found in the cold waters of South Africa, southern California, New Zealand, the Channel Islands, Australia, and Japan. Located close to the shore, abalone make their home on rocks or reefs. The red abalone is primarily located on the California coast.

MISSION NEARLY IMPOSSIBLE

Young abalone don't stand much of a chance in the wild. Once born, most are consumed by predators within twenty-four hours. Abalone that survive to reach adulthood can live up to forty years.

BODY ARMOR

Abalone shells are built to withstand hard blows. Scientists are studying them for ideas on how to build stronger body armor. An abalone shell's strength comes from its tiny tiles made of calcium carbonate that stack together like bricks. These tiles are held together with a type of protein glue.

21. AMMONITE

CLASSIFICATION

KINGDOM: *Animalia*

PHYLUM: *Mollusca*

CLASS: *Cephalopoda*

SUBCLASS: *Ammonoidea*

Ammonites were marine mollusks that lived about 66 million years ago. Fossils can still be found, and they are known for their tight coils. They were sometimes known as "snakestones" because they resemble coiled up snakes that had been turned to stone. Close relatives of cephalopods like squids and octopuses, ammonites had tentacles and swam with jet propulsion. But they also had shells made of a shiny, aragonite mineral, which provided some protection for their soft parts. It is believed that these mollusks lived for millions of years and evolved into all sorts of shapes and varieties over time. Their diet consisted mainly of plankton, which, if that plankton population was disrupted, might explain what led to the ammonite's eventual extinction.

WHERE TO FIND THEM

Ammonite fossils have been found all over the planet, from the Himalayas to Antarctic glaciers to the Great Plains of North America. You can find them almost anywhere oceans once existed, and especially at certain beaches where prehistoric fossil beds are revealed by low tide.

HOME ADDITIONS

Ammonites had a way to update and enlarge their homes to fit their growing bodies. Born with tiny shells, ammonites would build new chambers onto the shell as they grew. When a new, larger chamber was ready, they would move their entire body into it and seal off the old chamber. The wall to seal off the old chamber is known as a septa.

HELPFUL HISTORIANS

Ammonite shells are abundant and can be used as excellent index fossils. This means they can help scientists date other fossils that are found in the same layers of marine rock. They can also provide information about ancient climates, as their locations were once covered by ancient seas. Even cooler, the suture patterns on ammonite shells can help determine their species and time period!

22. MITRE

The mitre shell is the home to marine snails belonging to the *Mitridae* family. With over 500 species worldwide, they come in endless colors, patterns, and textures. While some are smooth with shallow ribbing, others have much more texture and well-defined ribbing along the spirals. All mitres have unique folds on their inside column, or columella, though this feature can only be observed if the shell is broken or if viewed by an x-ray. Another clue to help identify a mitre when shell hunting is that they have a narrow aperture (opening); it is only a quarter to half the shell's overall length.

CLASSIFICATION

KINGDOM: *Animalia*

PHYLUM: *Mollusca*

CLASS: *Gastropoda*

SUBCLASS: *Caenogastropoda*

ORDER: *Neogastropoda*

SUPERFAMILY: *Mitroidea*

FAMILY: *Mitridae*

WHERE TO FIND THEM
Mitres are usually found in temperate and tropical seas worldwide. They like to reside under rocks or just under the surface of the sand in intertidal water. However, they can also be found in water depths of up to 1,000 feet.

83

RELIGIOUS RESEMBLANCE

The mitre shell got its name from its resemblance to the ceremonial headdresses worn by Roman Catholic abbots and bishops. Interestingly enough, the Mitra mitra *(one of the largest mitre shells) also goes by the name of "Episcopal mitre."*

CAN YOU "SPOT" THE MITRE?

Just as cheetahs and giraffes are known by their spots, so are the Mitra mitra *and* Mitra papalis *shells. Both varieties have a pearly white shell covered with spirals of orange-brown spots. These mitres in particular are highly sought after by collectors.*

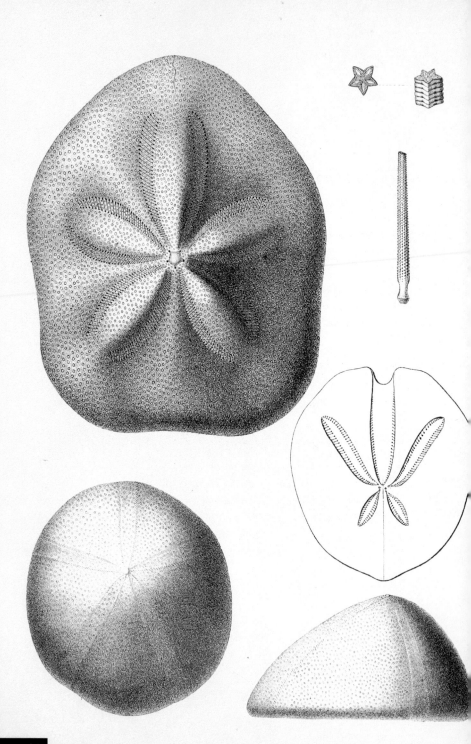

23. SAND DOLLAR

CLASSIFICATION

KINGDOM: *Animalia*

PHYLUM: *Mollusca*

CLASS: *Gastropoda*

SUBCLASS: *Caenogastropoda*

ORDER: *Neogastropoda*

SUPERFAMILY: *Mitroidea*

FAMILY: *Mitridae*

Though perhaps not a shell in the truest sense, no book would be complete without the sand dollar. Sand dollars are actually a type of sea urchin, and they've been called "sea biscuits," "sand cakes," and "cake urchins." Sand dollars are easily recognized by the characteristic five-petal shape on top of their disc-shaped skeleton, which is called a "test." When alive, sand dollars are covered in tiny spines, each of which are covered in even tinier hairs. These move in coordinated fashion and allow a sand dollar to scoot along the seabed—yes, they can move! When you find a sand dollar on the beach, you've usually come across the leftover test (the outside skeleton) sometime after the creature has died. Sand dollars come in a variety of colors, including purple, brown, blue, and green. The white sand dollars you find have usually been bleached by the sun.

WHERE TO FIND THEM
Sand dollars can be found worldwide but usually in temperate or warm waters. In the United States, they can be found on nearly all beaches along the continental shoreline.

ABOUT THE AUTHOR

Christin is the author of several books for kids. She lives with her family in California, where she enjoys rollerblading, puzzles, and a good book.

**BUSHEL
& PECK
BOOKS**

ABOUT THE
PUBLISHER

Bushel & Peck Books is a children's publishing house with a special mission. Through our Book-for-Book Promise™, we donate one book to kids in need for every book we sell. Our beautiful books are given to kids through schools, libraries, local neighborhoods, shelters, nonprofits, and also to many selfless organizations who are working hard to make a difference. So thank you for purchasing this book! Because of you, another book will find itself in the hands of a child who needs it most.

Printed in the United States
by Baker & Taylor Publisher Services